Wild Animals Coloring Book

40+ Coloring Pages of Audubon Illustrations of North American Wildlife, Including Wolf, Bear, Tiger, Deer, Bison…

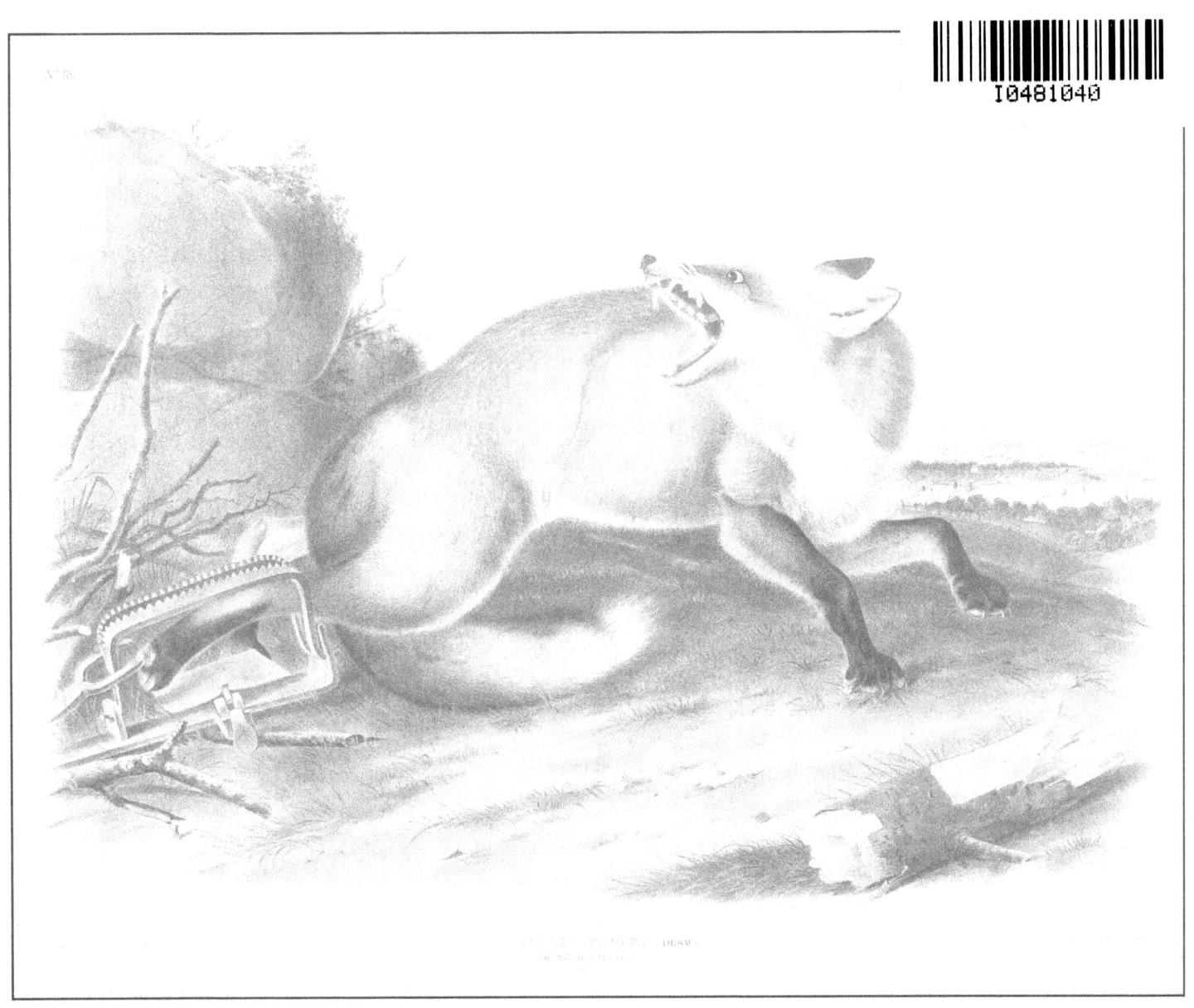

I0481040

Ada Ashley

©LeVintagePrintage

In this art coloring book, you will find 43 amazing illustrations by famous naturalist painter John James Audubon, reproduced true to original in light grayscale, perfect for realistic coloring and art therapy relaxation. Illustrations are reproduced without hard outlines for the opportunity to color them as actual artwork and be proud to cut out and display after finishing. In addition to coloring, this book allows you to practice drawing, shading, and tracing based on the artwork of a master illustrator. Coloring sheets are one-sided and blank on the back so they can be cut out for display or separate coloring.

Ada Ashleyw

PLATE CVI

PLATE. LXXI

CANIS LATRANS, s.w.
PRAIRIE WOLF.

PLATE LXXVI

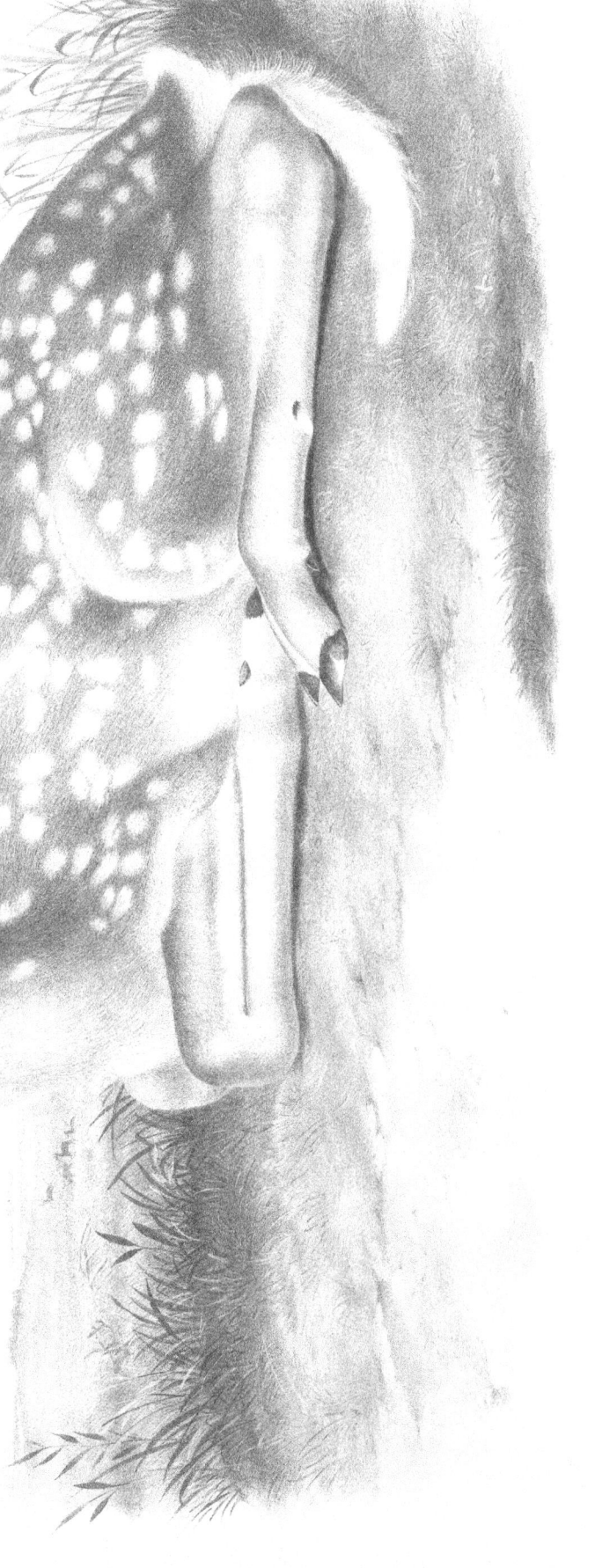

CERVUS (MACROTIS) PENNANT

FAWN. COMMON DEER.

PLATE CXXVI

TARANDUS RANGIFER Agassiz.

PLATE CXXVII

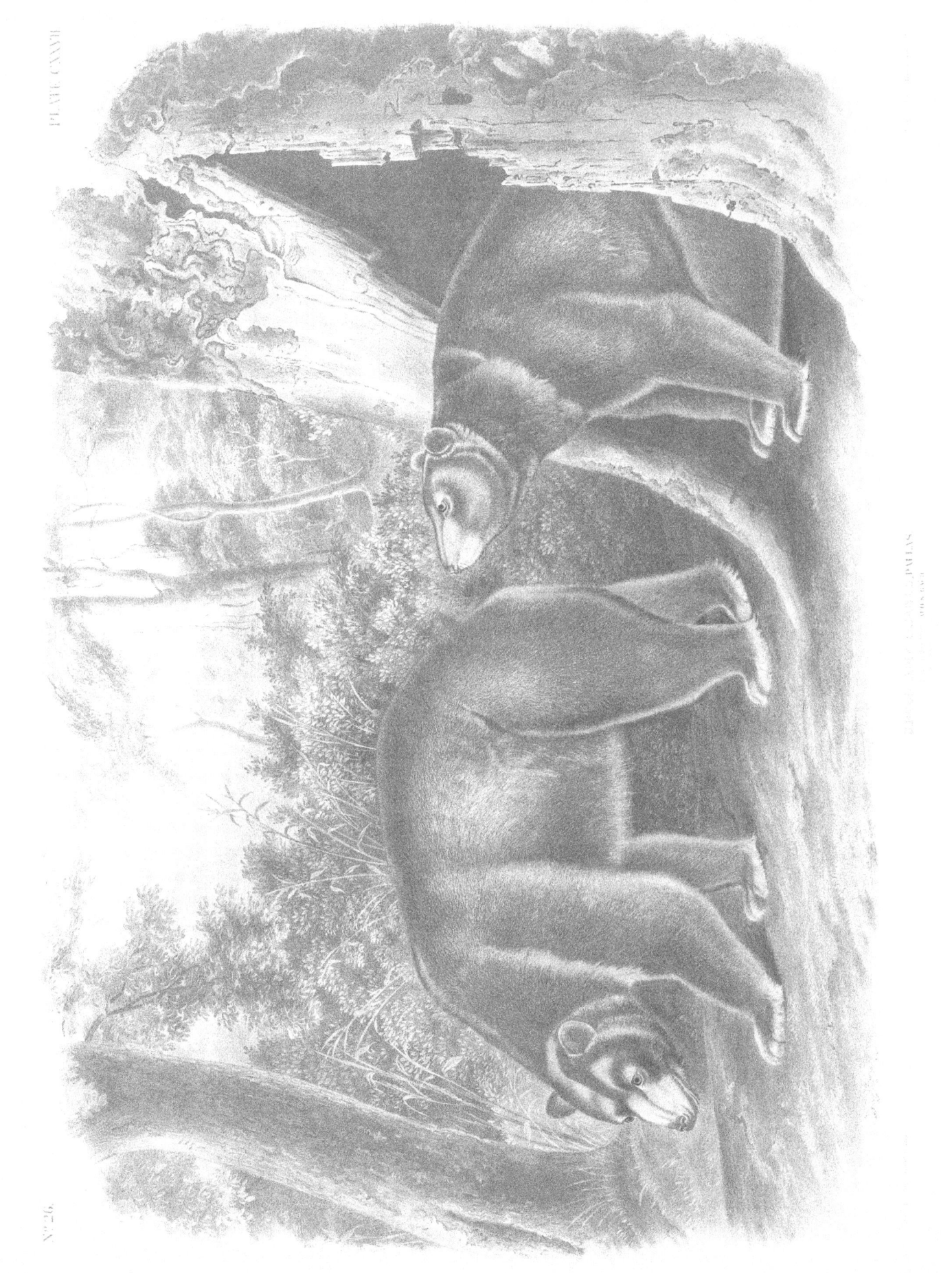

AMERICAN BLACK BEAR. — URSUS AMERICANUS, PALLAS.

PLATE I.

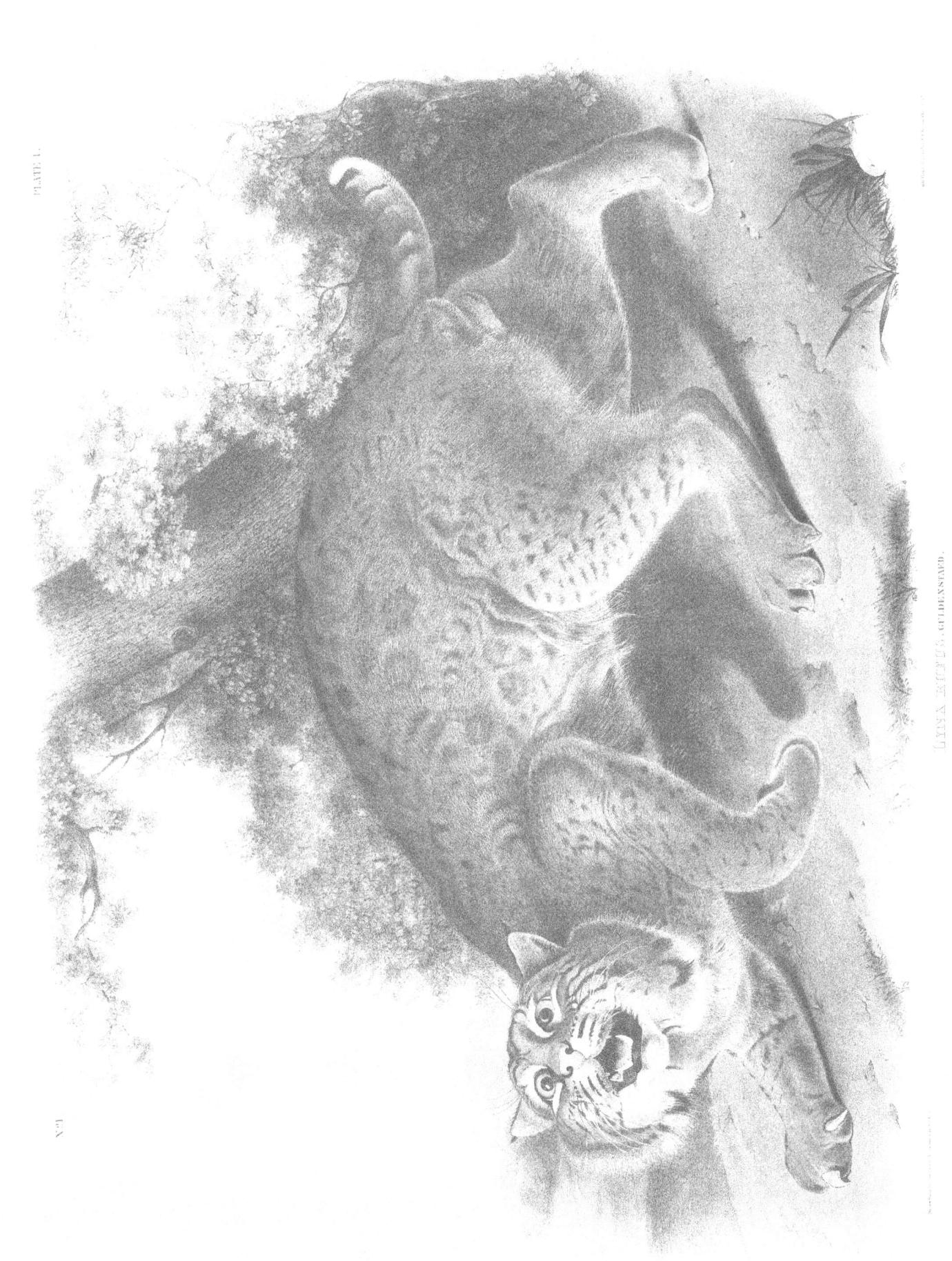

LYNX RUFUS, GULDENSTADT.
COMMON AMERICAN WILD CAT.

PLATE LXII

BOS AMERICANUS.
AMERICAN BISON OR BUFFALO.

PLATE CXXII

PETIT-BAIRONGUI SAEINDENSIS
PETAURISTA SABRINA, Gray

PLATE XI

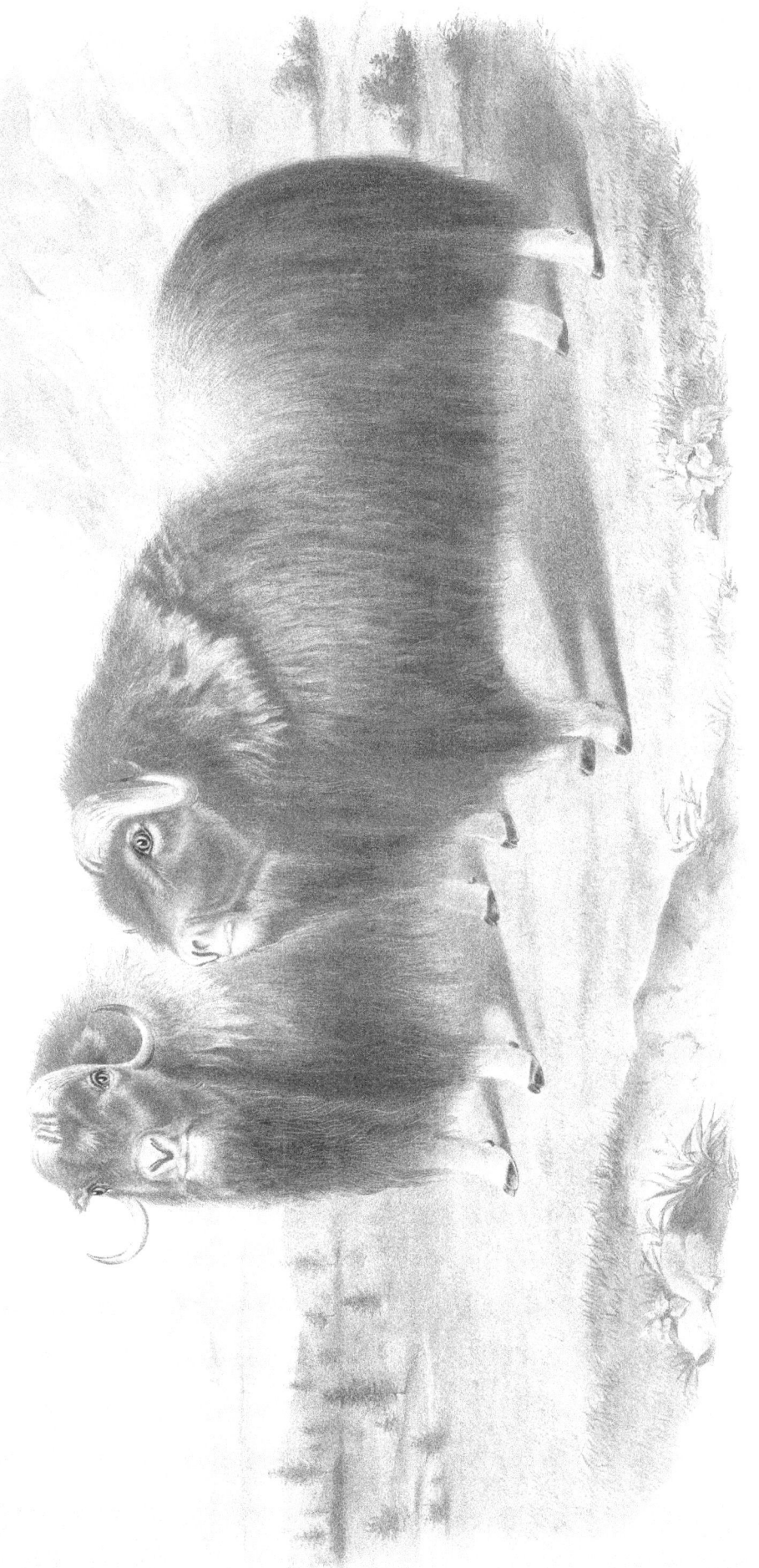

PLATE XXXVI

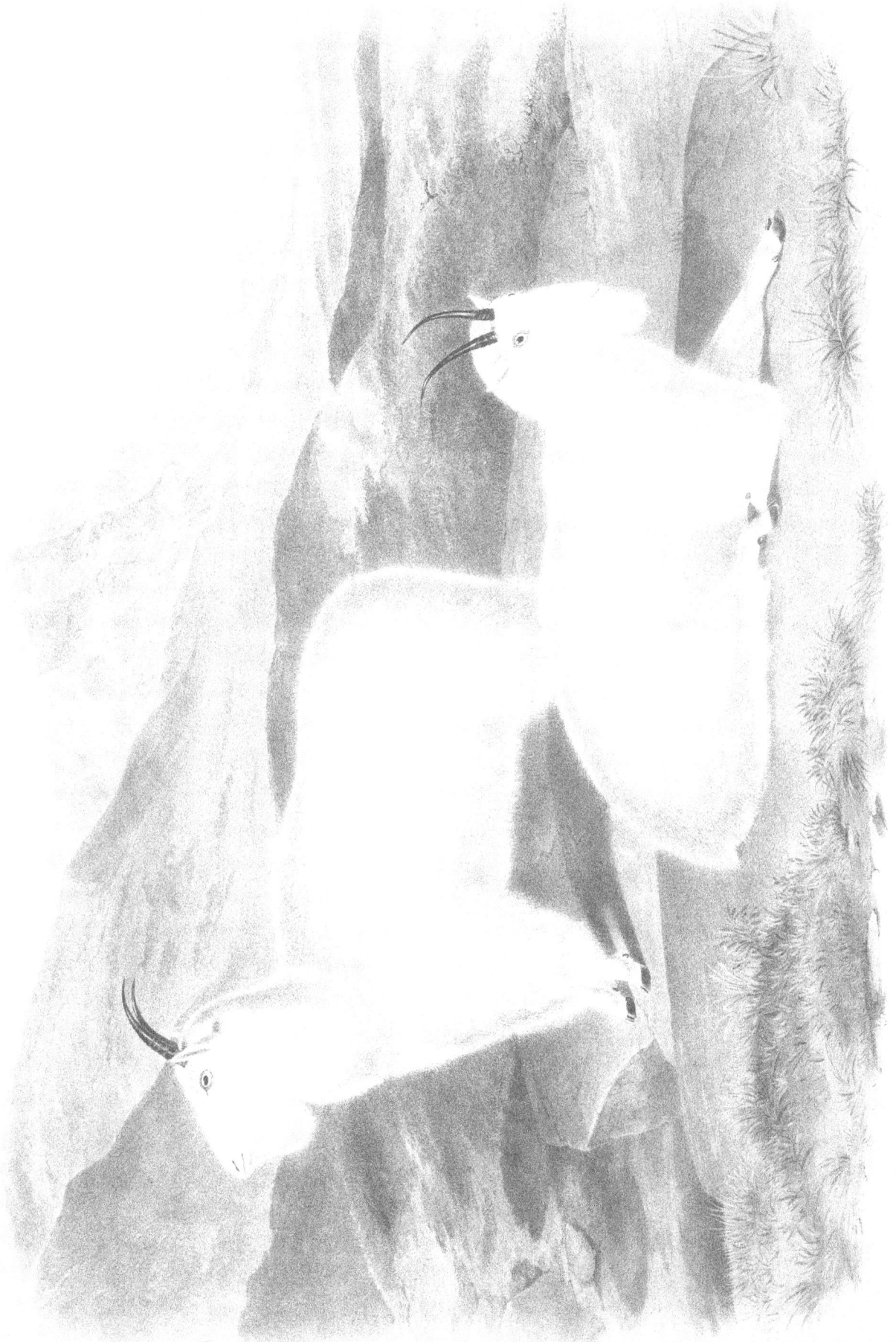

PLATE LXVI.

CANIS LUPUS LINN. VAR. NUBILUS

PLATE CXVIII

CERVUS LEUCURUS, DOUGLASS.
Long-tailed Deer.

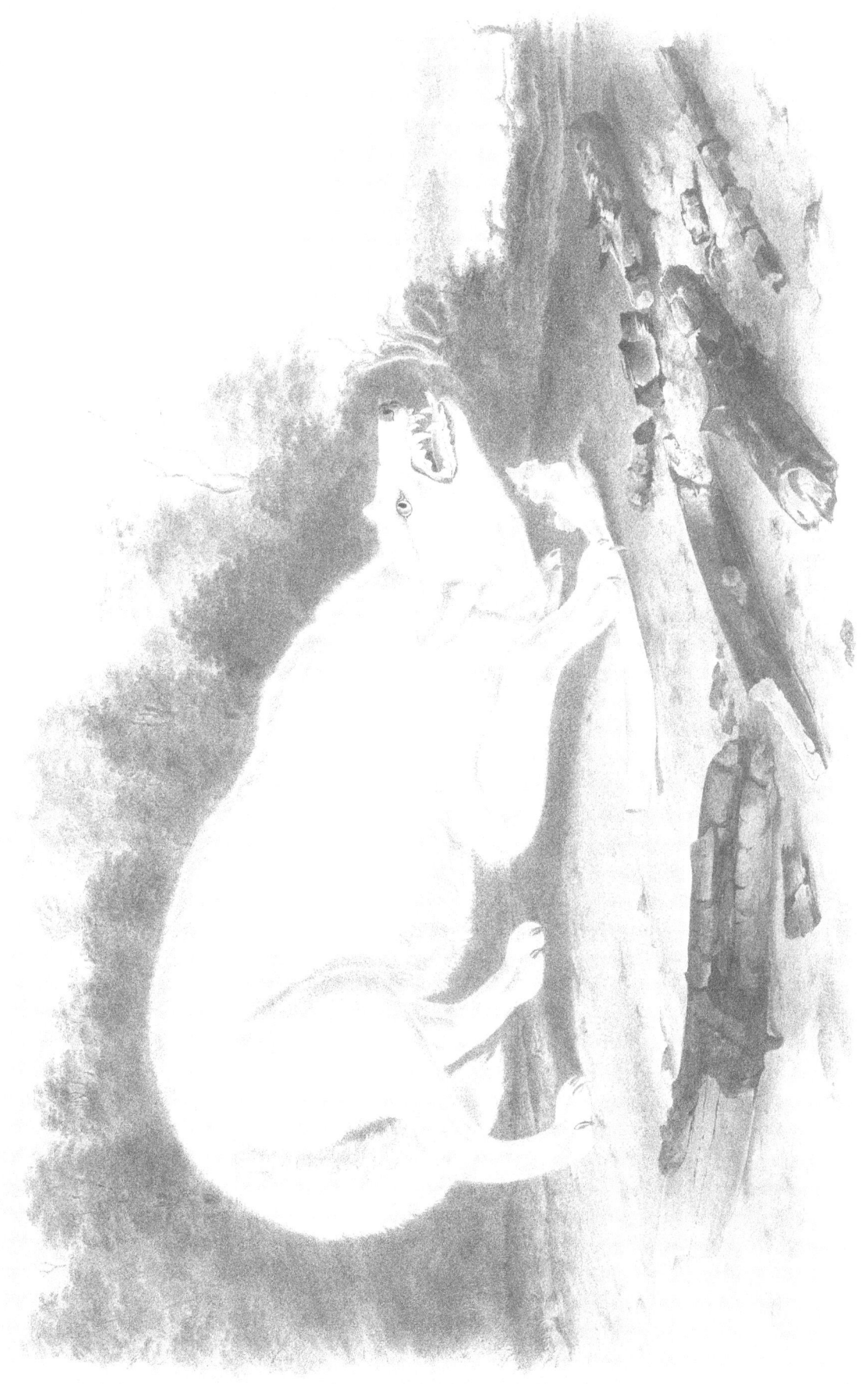

PLATE LXVI

CANIS (LUPUS) LYCAON VAR.
WHITE AMERICAN WOLF

PLATE LXXIII.

OVIS MONTANA. DESM.

PLATE LXXVIII.

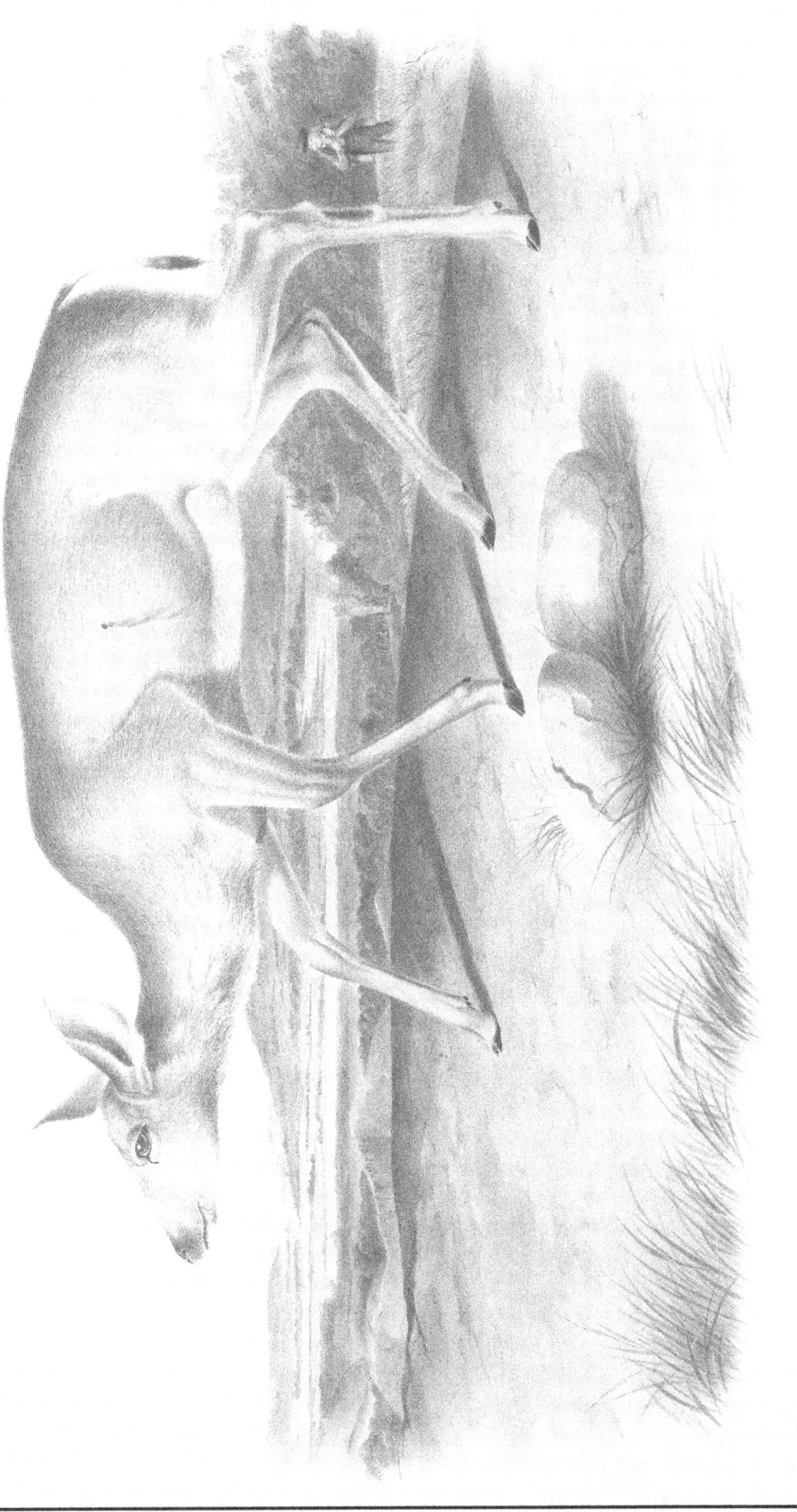

LEPUS TOWNSENDII. SAY

BLACK-TAILED HARE.

MALE & YOUNG FEMALE.

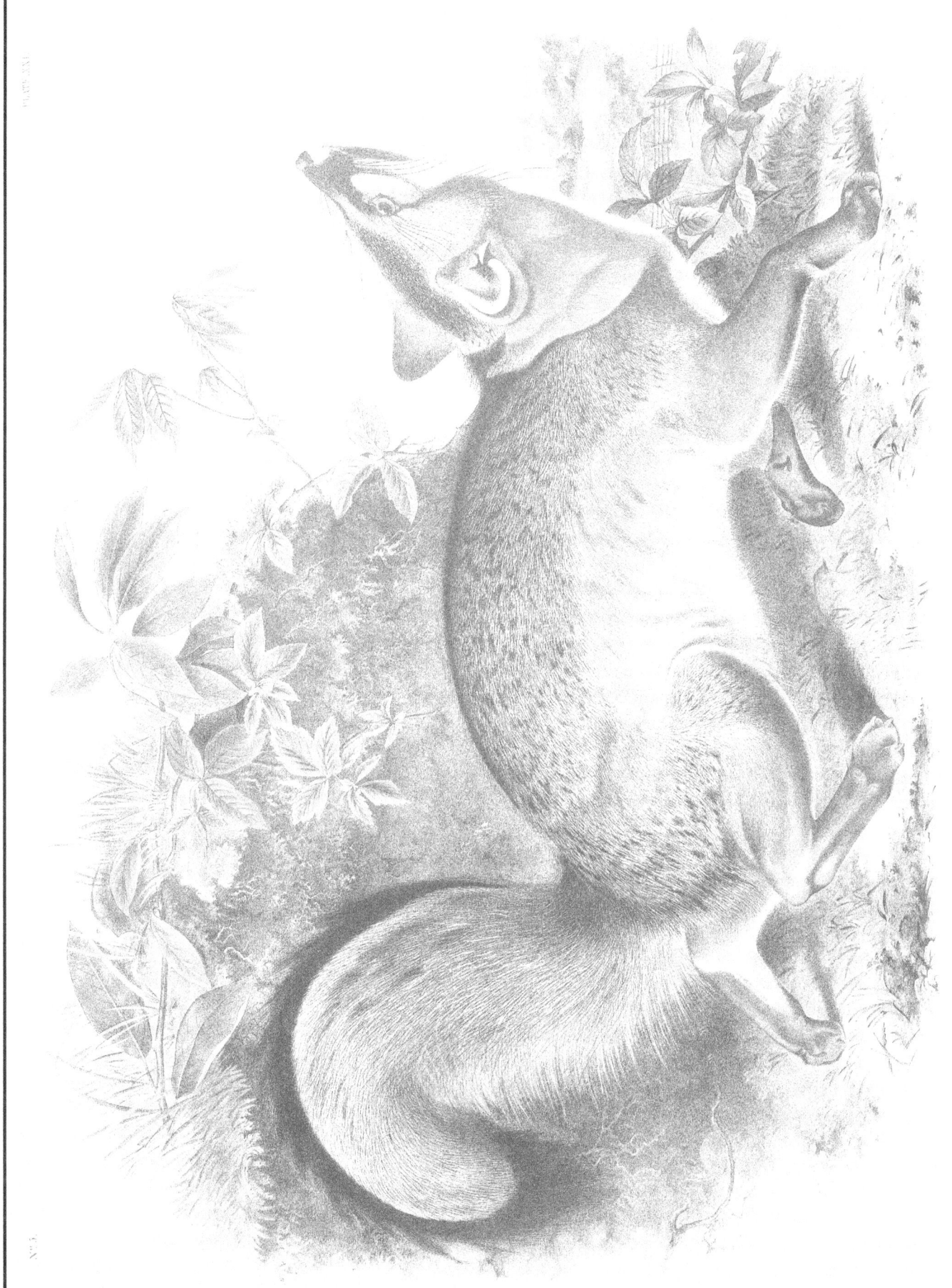

PLATE XCII.

LYNX LIBYCA, var. MACULATA. HORSFIELD & VIGORS.

PLATE XCVI.

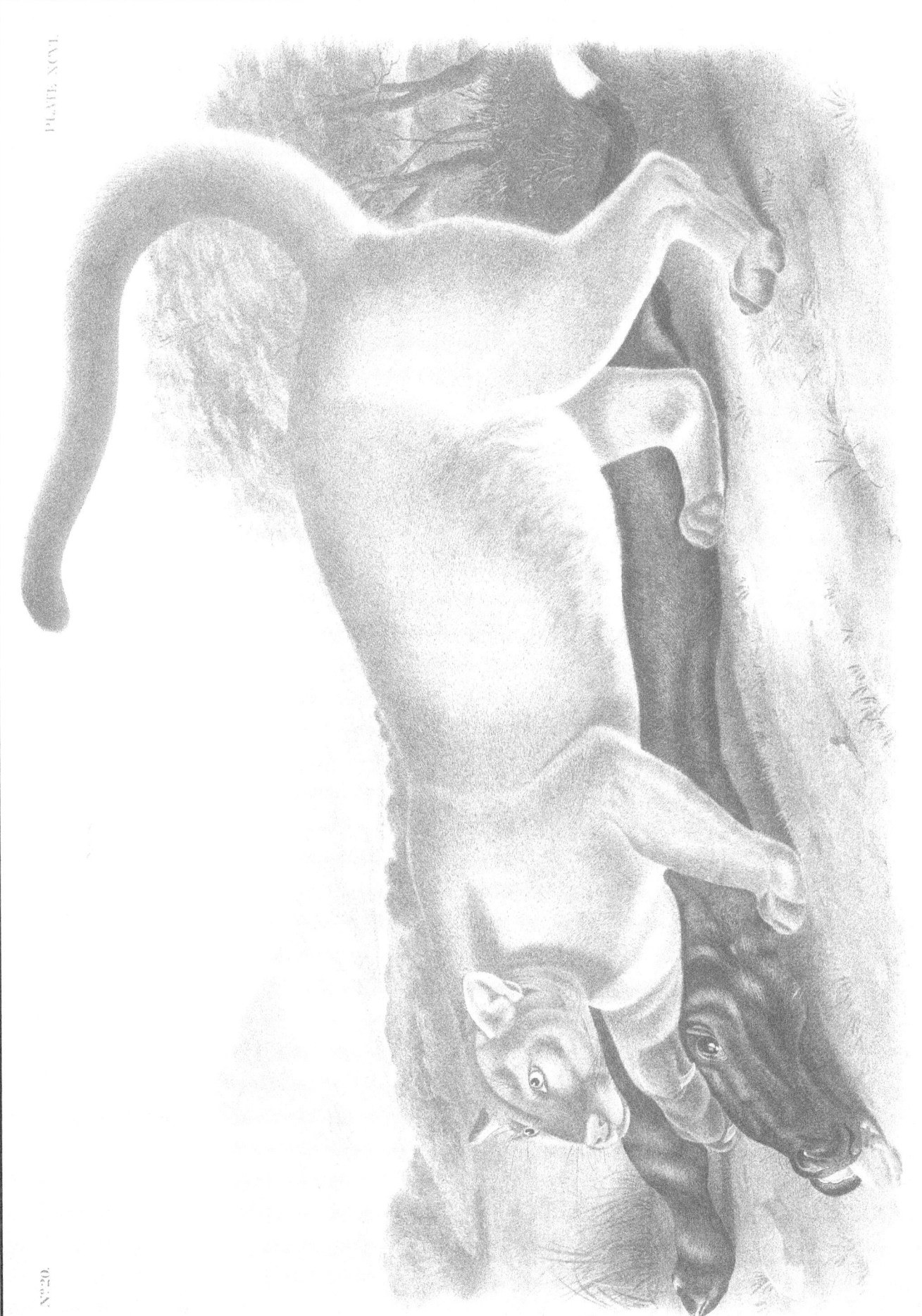

FELIS CONCOLOR, LINN.

PLATE LXXXI

PLATE XXVI

PLATE XXXVI.

PLATE LXXXI

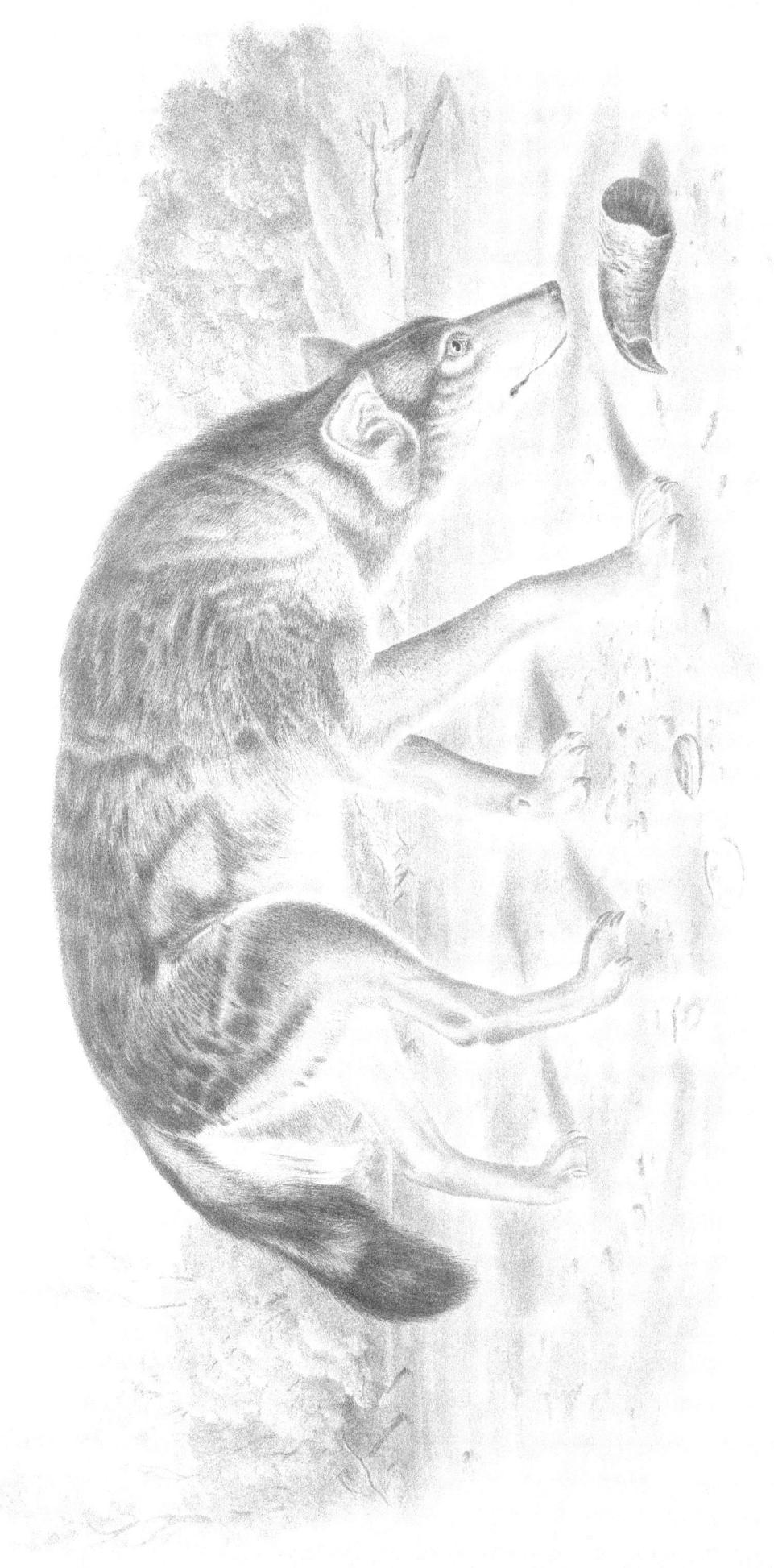

PLATE LXXXVII

PLATE CXXVII

PLATE XXVII

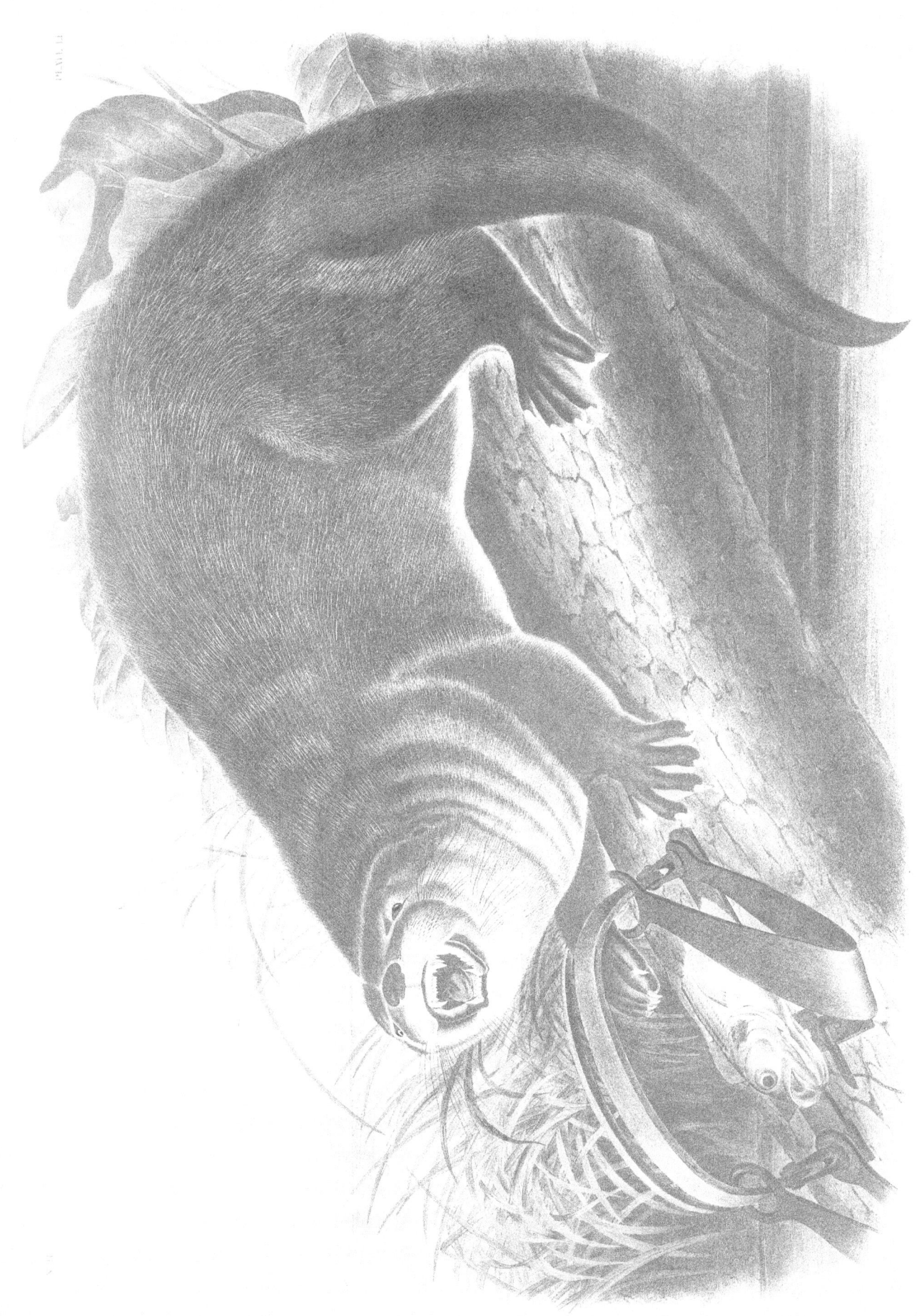

PLATE XCI.

URSUS MARITIMUS, LINN.
POLAR BEAR.

PLATE XCVII.

PLATE III.

VULPES VELOX, SAY.
SWIFT FOX.

PLATE VI.

CANIS VULPES (VAR.) FULVUS. DESMAREST.
AMERICAN RED FOX.
NAT. SIZE

PLATE CXVI

PLATE LXXVII.

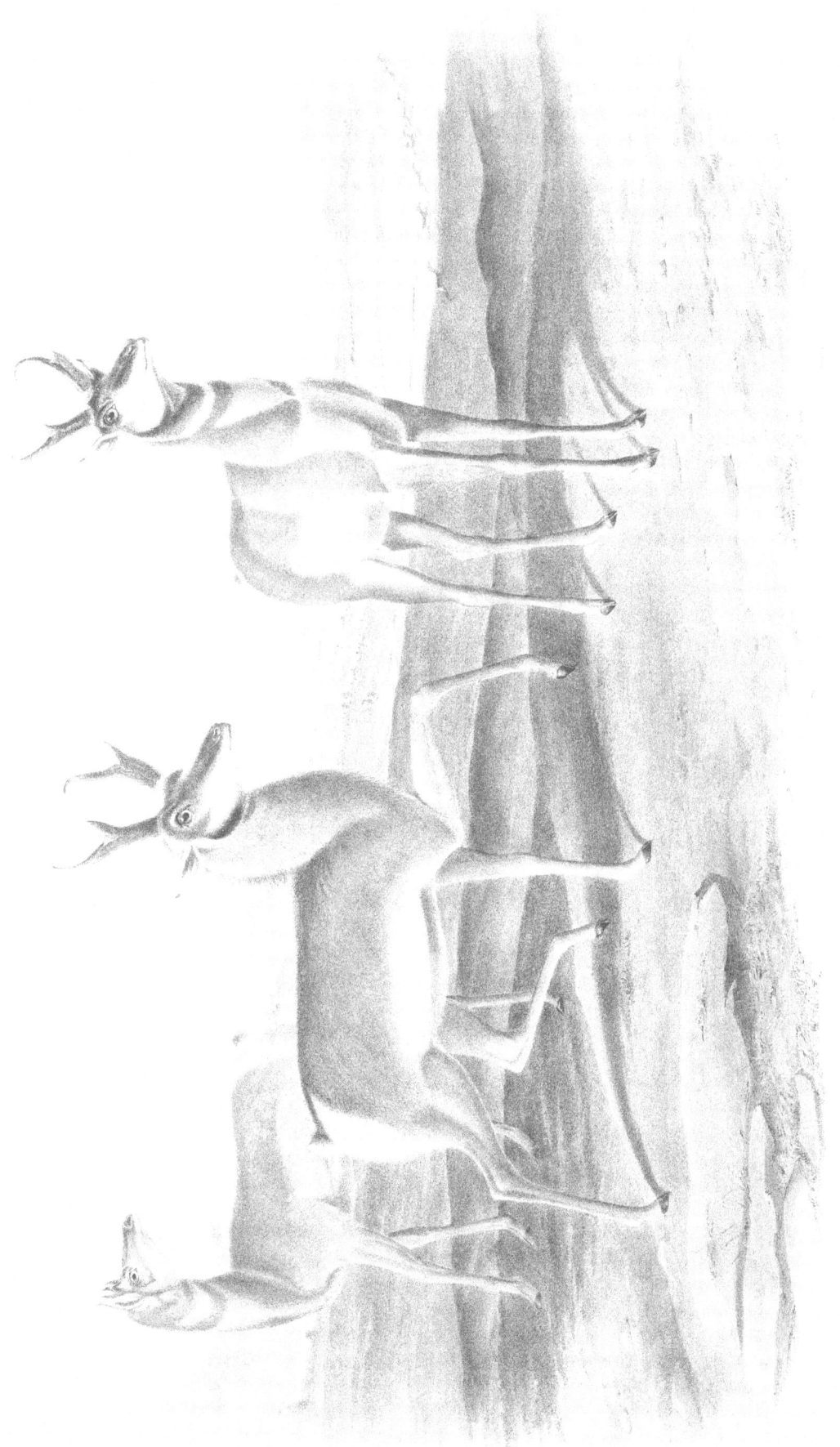

ANTILOPE AMERICANA (ORD.)

PLATE CXXXVI

PLATE LXVI

PLATE LVI.

BOS AMERICANUS, GML.

AMERICAN BISON OR BUFFALO.

Male.

PLATE LXI

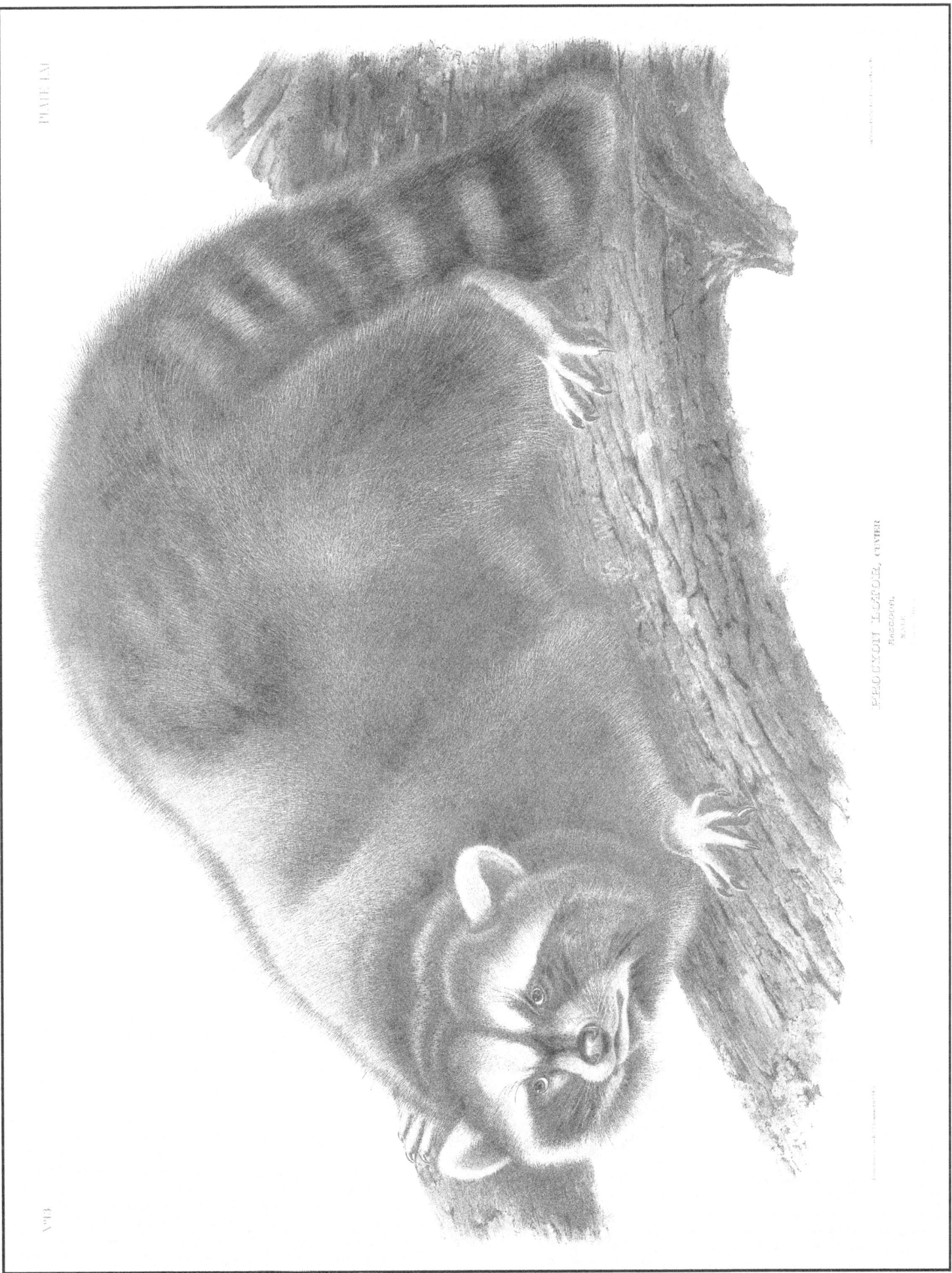

PROCYON LOTOR, Cuvier
RACCOON,
MALE

PLATE LVI

PROCYON LOTOR, Cuvier

RACCOON

MALE

PLATE CXIII.

CANIS FAMILIARIS, LINN. THE KRUSO HUSKY.

PLATE LXXXVI

FELIS PARDALIS, LINN.

THE LEOPARD CAT.

PLATE CXLI.

PLATE CI.

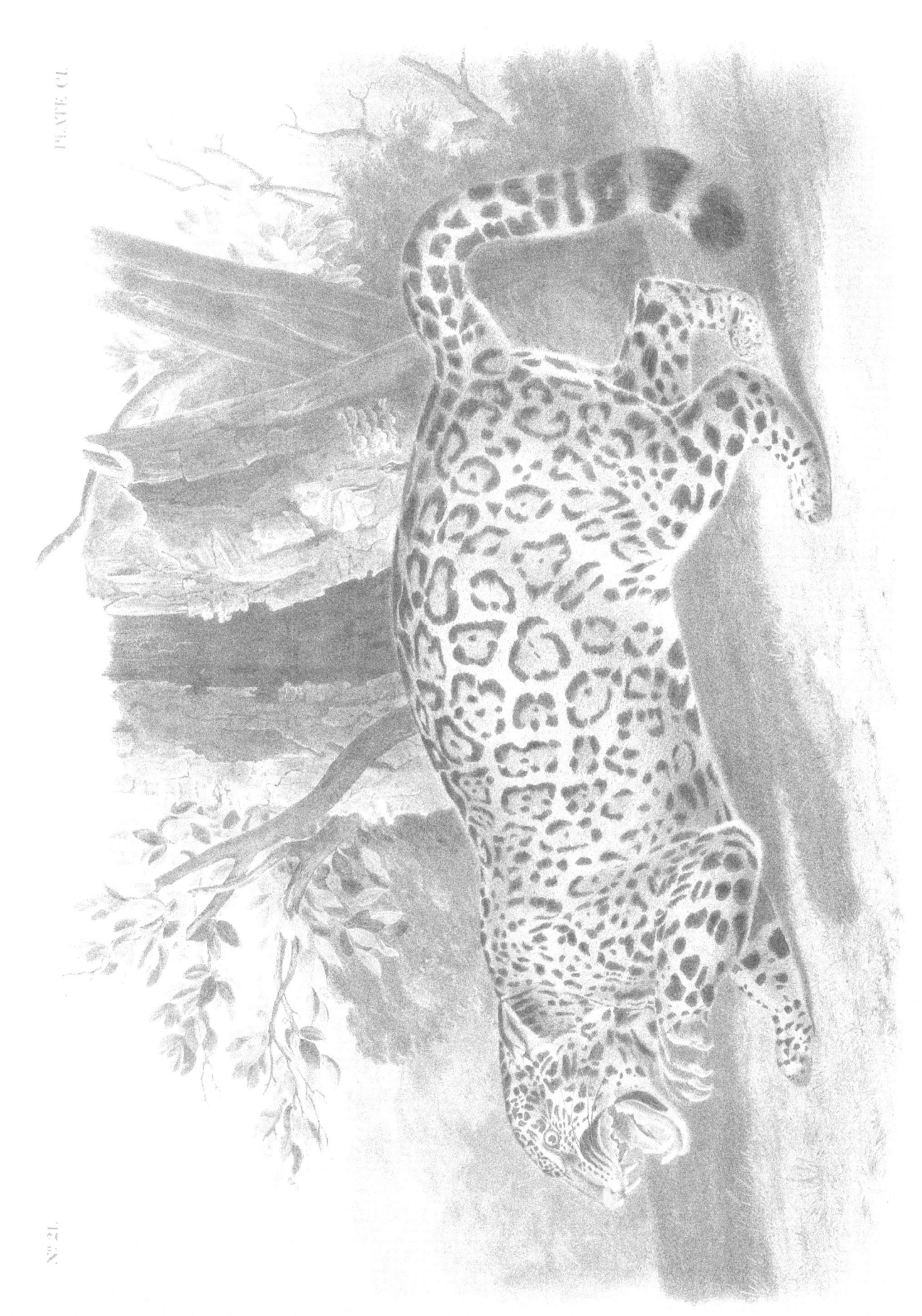

FELIS ONCA, LINN.
The Jaguar.

PLATE CI.

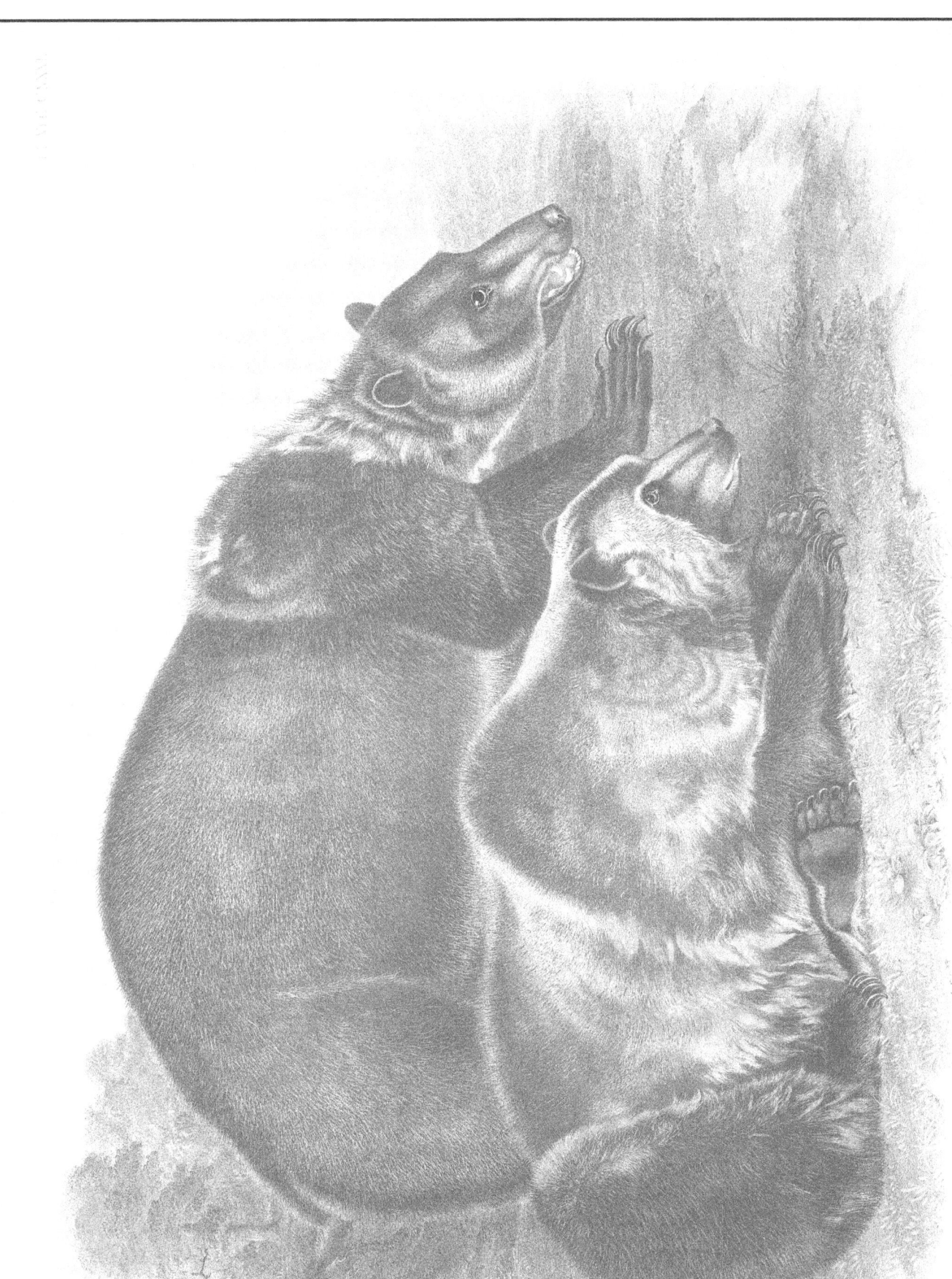